Money on the Altar

Dr. Marlene Miles

Freshwater Press 2024

ISBN: 978-1-963164-19-0

Paperback Version

Table of Contents

MONEY
ON
THE
ALTAR

Freshwater

What Is an Altar?

The word, *altar* comes from a Hebrew word which means, *to slay.* A place of slaughter. In today's vernacular, *to slay* means something totally different than what one might think. Nowadays, it means to greatly impress, to look so good that your appearance is so superlative that others must notice. It means your confidence will be through the roof, and over the moon.

The word, *altar* describes the physical structure, whereas the words, *to slay* describe what **happens** on that physical structure.

Altars were generally erected in conspicuous places, purposefully. An altar could look like anything, a flat piece of Earth, a stone or a rock. It could be made of wood, for example, the Cross on which Jesus was sacrificed. Yes, that was an altar, as was the wood that Isaac was secured to in his almost-sacrifice. The Word says that we are to take up *our* cross, **daily** --.

We worship God at an altar, we do not worship the altar. Jesus said to eat of His flesh and drink of His Blood to remember the Lord's death until He comes. He did not say to make replicas of the altar on which He was sacrificed to remember His death for décor or jewelry. Least of all do we use that altar with Jesus on the Cross, as He is no longer there.

Altars were erected by Noah, Abraham, Isaac, Jacob, Moses, among others. In the Bible, if you were having a sanctioned, proper relationship with God, an altar was involved.

Altars were public, they were set up as memorials and they were for the public to use. As long as an altar is godly it will have a known name, The Altar of Burnt Offering, the Brazen Altar, or the Table of the Lord, for example. The Altar of Incense was also called the Golden Altar. On this altar sweet spices were **continually** burned with fire taken from the Brazen Altar. The burning of the incense was a type of prayer And, there was the Altar of Wood These were named altars, so they were known to the people.

On these altars, they offered the blood of bulls and goats. Since the Better Blood of Jesus Christ, we offer our own bodies as a living sacrifice, which is our reasonable act of worship (Rom 12:1-2).

Israel brought the Lord: the burnt offering, the grain offering, the peace offering, the sin offering and the trespass offering. There was a specific reason for each type of sacrifice. Along with the burnt offering, offered twice each day, was the grain offering of flour, oil, frankincense, and salt, which expressed gratitude to God and served as a way of asking the Lord to remember the worshipper with favor (Leviticus 2).

The regular burnt offering was to be performed every day of the year, so all other sacrifices were in addition to it (Num 28–29). These were the foundation of sacrifices to God.

People of God, hear this… the sacrifices placed on the altars in Bible time were continuous, some were 24/7, some were daily, some prn. However, if we note what was sacrificed it was food. It was the food they enjoyed. So there was a sweet smelling aroma going up to God at all times, and it smelled good to the worshippers as well, yet they had to resist the temptation to partake of it, to eat it, to consume it, themselves.

Command Aaron and his sons, saying,
This is the law of the burnt offering.
The burnt offering shall be on the
hearth on the altar all night until the
morning, and the fire of the altar shall
be kept burning on it. (Leviticus 6:9)

And this is the law of the grain
offering. The sons of Aaron shall offer
it before the LORD in front of the altar.

And one shall take from it a handful of
the fine flour of the grain offering and
its oil and all the frankincense that is
on the grain offering and burn this as
its memorial portion on the altar, a
pleasing aroma to the LORD.

And the rest of it Aaron and his sons
shall eat. It shall be eaten
unleavened in a holy place. In the
court of the tent of meeting they shall
eat it.

It shall not be baked with leaven. I
have given it as their portion of my
food offerings. It is a thing most holy,

like the sin offering and the guilt offering.

Every male among the children of Aaron may eat of it, as decreed forever throughout your generations, from the LORD's food offerings. Whatever touches them shall become holy."
(Leviticus 6:)

Saints of God, do not complain that the pastor is getting a portion of the offerings on the altar; that is allowed and mandated by God. Further, this is his job. If someone told you to come to work and do your job but you are not getting paid, would you go? If you were told to come to work but you may or may not get paid, would you go? Do you serve a God who is too cheap or too broke to pay His servants?

Then you cannot disparage the pastors of God getting paid.

Any man given to appetite smelling all those aromas all day and night, Proverbs 23:2) --, it had to be hard on him, but it was a test of his holiness, faithfulness and it helped him to suppress greed. Delayed gratification builds soul prosperity.

While in college, I lived about a block away from a cookie factory. I smelled cookies every day and I could tell you what flavor cookies were baking on any given day. Temptation? Yes. Did I give in and go to the store and get cookies? From time to time, but after a while I got over it, Amen.

In the other direction, a bit further away there was, and still is a spice and condiment company. If the wind was right, I could smell black pepper being packaged. On some days I could smell cinnamon. Barbeque sauce was being bottled on other days. It was an olfactory festival around that area.

Chefs always say that people eat with their eyes, which is why the serpent had Eve to *look* at the apple. Please know this, smell is a very important factor in appetite and the taking of meals. Smelling food can be a great temptation to man.

In addition, food is a gateway drug. Yes, I said that. I mean it too. A man who is given to appetite gives in to his wants, desires, and lusts. Often that is the same man who will chase women, drugs, alcohol--, anything he wants he believes he has the right to get and partake of--, *now*. Believe me, the choosier man can be trusted more.

Now, that gets us to fasting – this is another reason why we fast; it is to bring the flesh under submission. We are telling the flesh you cannot have everything you want, when you want it. Fasting is a discipline, and it is easier for the already disciplined soul. For the soul that is not disciplined, fasting creates discipline.

Saints of God if **you** don't want what you're putting on the altar, it wouldn't be a sacrifice. If you don't want it, why do you think God would? If it is something that you have no use for, or no longer have use for, it is not a sacrifice. It's on the altar, it looks good, smells good and you get to partake of something like it from time to time, so you definitely know how it tastes.

But you let it go because it is an offering. You let it go because it is a sacrifice. This is why it says in the Word that offerings are given of our free will. If someone has to MAKE, coerce, urge, trick, blackmail or guilt you into "giving", that's not giving, it is robbery or witchcraft.

Offerings are not as if you're cleaning out your garage and going to Goodwill. God is not brought your leftovers or discards. What are we talking about here? Goodwill doesn't even accept damaged donations. If it is, however, something you can use and would desire but you are letting go of it, that is an offering and it is an offering of love if you are presenting it in love, in obedience and with the right spirit to honor the Lord.

Why An Altar?

An altar is the interface between the physical realm and the spiritual realm. Altars are places of power. The enemies of God knew that if they destroyed their opponents' altars they'd render them powerless.

Do you have an altar? Do you service an altar? Do you sacrifice on a Godly altar? If not, the enemy has convinced you either that you don't need one or that the one that is available to you is futile.

In the Bible, enemies stole and polluted Godly altars. In the Bible the Israelites took altars back from the enemies and reconsecrated them for

Godly use again. The Bible recounts many altar wars, one of great significance is the loss, the capturing and the returning of the Ark of the Covenant. God judged kings in the Bible by how they either treated His altars, if they let God's altars be captured or desecrated, God did not look so favorably on them.

Kings were acknowledged by God as "good" for tearing down the enemy's evil altars because those evil altars abounded in the "high places." Even today, altars in high places are many. We are told in the Bible to pluck up, tear down and rout the enemy's altar.

If we disrupt what happens at an enemy's altar, we break their source of power, render them powerless and God wins. We win when God wins, Amen.

But know, that is exactly what the enemy is doing to the saints of God – trying to keep them away from Godly altars, interfere with their worship and sacrifice, or destroy Godly altars.

People think the way to God is through religion – it is not. It is dedicated worship to God through a Godly altar. Of course, to *priest* at an altar, one must be qualified to *priest*, by living in consecration and holiness. *Who* is reaching out to God is as important as **how** it is being done.

Phineas and Hophni, Eli's kids were not living consecrated before the Lord, they were sleeping with the temple prostitutes. They were slain by the Lord.

Temple prostitutes were common in that day and from the looks of some at some churches--, even now.

Nadab & Abihu offered strange fire before the Lord, and the Lord consumed them.

Saints of God, what's your level of consecration as you priest, or minister at <u>any</u> Godly altar? Are you serious, or are you just playing with God? God is not playing with us. You don't offer strange fire before the Lord, do you?

You don't roll out of a bed of fornication, for example, with someone who is not your covenant spouse and take a sacrifice to a godly altar, *do you*? Neither do you live in holiness but take a blemished sacrifice to the Lord. *Right*?

In the tabernacles of the Lord, the priests could not enter into the Holy of Holies. and live unless he was sin free and had lived in holiness for the entire year previous. Priests went into the Holy of Holies, where the Presence of God was with a rope tied around their ankles so if they didn't come out in a certain time frame, that meant they had died, and had to be dragged or pulled out of there.

It is God's Mercy that keeps us OUT of the Presence of God because you're not getting in if you are riddled with sin; this is why we must repent. That's Mercy because **a blemished priest is as bad or worse than a blemished offering, but a blemished offering is really bad.**

Not one of us should have so much temerity to try to enter into the Holy of Holies, the very Presence of God—to His altar, where we want to meet up with God without at least trying to live holy and bringing a proper sacrifice, not a blemished, half-way, kinda-sorta type offering.

Which Altar?

There are godly altars and there are dark, evil, witchcraft and satanic altars.

You have been giving offerings on an altar of some kind even if you think you have not been.

Idols demand worship and they will trick you to get it if necessary. The Holy Spirit is a gentleman and will always ask you first, wait for a response or your approval before initiating any covenant with man.

Of course, never expect a Godly altar in a satanic place. There is no worship of God in a nightclub, bar, or strip joint. But those places are themselves altars and the people who go there are the sacrifices. The alcohol, drugs, sex are all sins to open doors for the sinners and would-be sinners to be compromised by the devil, to later be sacrificed.

There can be altars within altars in these clubs. The workers, the customers, the narcissists – they are all altars and are trying to garner, demand, or force worship from humans. As I've said before, if you've never met one, you might *be* one.

Where an altar is located may tell a lot about what type of altar it is; evil altars are in evil places—high places, evil forests or groves, satanic and idolatrous locations. Additionally, because man is deceptive – and so is the devil, an evil altar could be in an otherwise Godly place.

A church comes to mind, where we should be under the Grace of a pastor, if he is an occultic or satanic pastor, we are instead under whatever powers he is under. If he is a satanic pastor, he has no mercy. That is one of the hallmarks of a satanic pastor – he has no mercy. He has little to no fruit of the Spirit.

Any *fruit* you may see displayed in a false pastor is plastic, in a plastic bowl, on a plastic table, with a plastic tablecloth. Discern every *spirit* and believe the Holy Spirit when He speaks to you. If weird things are happening in that place, don't ignore those happenings.

Some years ago, the Lord gave me a dream of a known pastor (not well known), but locally known who was wearing white preaching robes. In the dream he was laughing heinously and saying, *"They usually wear black for this, I'm wearing white."*

When an altar is not erected in a conspicuous place, when one is deliberately hidden, suspect evil. Suspect the occult, since that word literally means, *hidden.* Sometimes hidden means behind something, under something, but sometimes it is hidden as in a masquerade, where there is the façade of something over something that the owners do not want the people to see. That evil altar could have a name, but it is not commonly known since the owners and operators of that altar want it to remain *occultic.*

There are evil altars masquerading as churches. There are evil altars under some churches. There are evil altars that are the source of power for some false and evil pastors. Unless they are doing things that are so evil, so dark, so brazen, so obviously **not** of God in there, the only way you will know for sure is to pray and ask the Holy Spirit.

Discern.

Listen to the set man of that house – what does he or she say or don't say? Do they preach on sin? Do they mention the Name of Jesus much, or at all? Do they ever preach on the Blood of Jesus? Do they preach from the Word? Do they recommend you read your own Bible for yourself? If they don't, if they are not clearly preaching Christ, and Him crucified, and the full Word of God, those are demonic or false pastors; you should not be there. And, their altars are no place you should ever put a nickel, a dime, or a dollar.

A lot of the time those are the churches where the pastor is asking for money and offerings all the time. If he or she is not teaching on the full Word of God, to include altars and the *why* of giving, you need to walk circumspectly. Discern every *spirit*. Especially notice if since you've been there you've been going down, instead of up. Have you been giving and giving, and living right before the Lord, but your finances are drained? How's your health? How's family life --, are your children doing well? Pray sincerely and ask God if you are supposed to stay there. In a proper church you should be edified, grow, experience lift, and your family should be prospering. If you are being drained instead, that is the sign of occultism. There's an evil altar there, and you are the sacrifice.

Evil sacrifice doesn't always happen all at once. Sometimes, it is by degrees. If you are not discerning, you may miss how good things in your life, such as peace, health, and wealthy are gradually ebbing from you.

Discern!

No, this is not paranoia; this is paying attention, this is discernment. Do not stay in any place so long that you are completely drained of life, health, resources, joy, and happiness. Especially don't stay there while your children are losing or suffering.

If you have ever given on a false altar, a strange altar, a satanic altar, an occultic altar, a witchcraft altar, a heathen altar, a pagan altar you need to both repent and also call your offerings back from that altar and plead the Blood of Jesus over what you put into the hands of an ungodly "priest."

You may say you never have. Really? Ever had your palm read? A tarot reading, has a fortune teller or astrologer read your future to you? And you paid them? Those are witchcraft altars.

Certain restaurants have their idols at the cash register – not only did you eat there – you ate food sacrificed to idols, but you also PAID money on their altar. Those are the obvious altars that you may have been oblivious to. Imagine the hidden altars that you didn't even know existed, and before today may not have believed they existed, even if someone told you.

Do not dedicate your hands to an idolatrous altar by continuing to go to certain nail salons---, and paying them! You are putting your hands in their hands and your money on the altars of the idols that they worship. The work of your hands for your entire life should be dedicated to God and those anointed hands should be bringing your sacrifices to the Altars of Jehovah God.

Altar Sacrifices

God has told man from the times of Cain and Abel what is appropriate as a sacrifice. He has indicated what is a sweet-smelling aroma, and He has indicated when, as well as having established the *where*.

Most often the instrument we use appears to be *financial*, but it isn't actually – it is the representation of our life. It is a SACRIFICE.

Pay your tithes and give offerings. Now, I'm not here to argue about tithes – I am teaching what is in my Bible. You do what God tells you to do. But, know this – the devil loves to trip humans up on technicalities…

YOU DO WHAT GOD TELLS YOU TO DO. As for me and my house we will serve the Lord and follow what is in the Holy Writ as much as it is possible, in the Name of Jesus. Amen.

God talks about sacrifice throughout the Bible. Abel offered a sacrifice of the firstlings of his flock (Genesis 4:4). God decided which animals were suitable for sacrifice and at what times they could or should be offered up.

Cain, in the fullness of time brought in his offering to God, but it was rejected. Most postulate that what Cain brought to God was rejected. That's a possibility, but it is the phrase, *the fullness of time* that attracts my attention. So, I believe that the **timing** of one's offering is also very much a part of whether it will be acceptable to God, or not.

So, my friends, if God decided what was an acceptable sacrifice and what was not, how is it that we think we can, ourselves, decide what is good or okay to bring, and when? Didn't Cain already do that? And, do you recall how that worked out for Cain? Cain's behavior after having his offering rejected by God is a clue as to the *spirit* or *spirits* in Cain. What **spirits** are in a man influences how he thinks and colors his decisions. If man has other *spirits* in him instead of The Holy Spirit, how can that man make the correct decision of what to bring God for an offering, and when? Other *spirits* are in a person's soul to influence that man or woman, and they can be very chatty. Do you think they will tell a person to do what God wants them to do? Of course, not; they will be led to do the opposite.

Therefore, unless a man is completely filled with the Holy Spirit, he cannot be wise enough, loving enough, holy enough or anything enough to know the right thing to sacrifice on a Godly altar. Until he knows how to hear from and obey the Holy Spirit, he must be told.

In the Bible, which is our model, sacrifices were either bloody or unbloody. Bloody offerings were burnt offerings, peace offering, and sin and trespass offerings. Unbloody offerings were such as the tithe, first fruits, and incense. You may think that none of this has anything to do with you. It does; the Bible is our model. If it is not to tell us what to do, it is at least for understanding.

- Sin offering, for access to God;

- Burnt offering, shows dedication.

- Meat offering, for thanksgiving.

Burnt offerings were made daily and constantly. What are you rendering unto the Lord, daily? What's on your altar, daily? There was a double burnt offering on the Sabbath. Burnt offerings were indicated for the festivals that God established for Israel. There were daily meat offerings to go with the daily burnt offerings, yet we know folks who complain about any offering declaring, *"That pastor only wants my money."*

Believing or discerning that the pastor only wants your money may mean that your spirit man is picking up on something wrong about that pastor or that church. It does not mean that there is anything wrong with God. In all your discerning, discern if that is the Holy Spirit talking to your spirit, or are there other *spirits* in there to lead you away from a godly altar that will minister to you and your family? Discern.

The temple shewbread was renewed every Sabbath, and there were extra meat offerings on that day. Bring ye meat into my storehouse... Malachi 3.

- Passover -First fruits.
- Pentecost – First fruits
- Sin offering each new moon.
- Sin offerings at the Passover, Pentecost, Feast of Trumpets and Tabernacles,
- The offering of the two goats for the people and of the bullock for the priest himself, on the Day of Atonement, Yom Kippur.
- Morning and evening incense and on the Day of Atonement.

Besides these public sacrifices, there were offerings of the people for themselves, individually. If this seems like a lot of offerings, you cannot deny that when you love someone, you *give*.

It's only natural. Even if you pull that Christmas stunt that I did one year where I only gave gifts to people who visited me---, GOD is Omnipresent, He is ever with you and your appropriate sacrifices will draw His attention and keep Him with you.

The sin offering was for covenant broken by man, needed to be repaired by God. In 2 Chronicles 29:21 seven bulls, seven rams, seven lambs and seven he-goats were sacrificed on the command of King Hezekiah for the kingdom, for the sanctuary, and for Judah; that was a sin offering.

People sacrificed at an altar to acknowledge God, make covenant, restore or renew covenant, seek the favor of God.

Money In the Temple

Worship was by a contribution, mostly an animal sacrifice. Nowadays, who do you know who will bring a whole animal to church for the altar? How about a ephah of flour or grain?

Jesus gave His Blood that we don't have to bring blood to the altar anymore. We may tender the sacrifice of Christ as our blood sacrifice, our grain offering, our sin offering, our peace offering and for thanksgiving.

In Exodus 30:13 and 38:25 it is commanded that every male over the age of 20 must give an annual contribution to the temple, of half a shekel. *How much is that?* In Bible days a *shekel* was about 14 grams of silver—a little less than half a Troy ounce, so a half a shekel therefore would be about 7 grams of silver. In today's market 7 grams of silver is approximately ¼ Troy ounce of silver –worth about $6.00.

A similar silver coin that Jesus spoke about was the wages of a day's work, one denarius, so a half a shekel would be worth about 2 days of labor in a vineyard. That would be about $75 now.

Jesus didn't praise the $1000 Line folks, He praised the widow woman who gave a mite, the smallest denomination of money of that time. We realize now that the widow's mite was an amazing offering because men usually gave their wives money for the offerings. The widow had no one to give her money for "church." Therefore, we may surmise that she gave of her own free will, she gave out of obedience and love. God looks at the heart of man.

Money on the Altar

The sacrifice nowadays is currency of paper and other metals. Currency has evolved through the generations. It's been salt, shells, grain, cattle, goats, silver, gold, bronze, iron. It still is silver and gold at Fort Knox, backing up paper currency, at least in this country.

Sacrifices on Godly altars are beautiful, to this writer, but mostly it should be attractive and inviting to God. Money on a Godly altar, to me, looks like the tents of Jacob in array, worshipping the LORD. This is not because it is currency or money, because

I don't, we don't worship money. It is beautiful because of what it represents. It represents **life--, the life** of the saints of God.

HOW GOODLY ARE THY TENTS, O JACOB, AND THY TABERNACLES, O ISRAEL! (NUMBERS 24:5)

To someone such as myself who operates in a prophetic grace – the sacrifices **are supposed to be there**. The sacrifices are **supposed** to be on that Godly altar. If the currency of sacrifice is *currency* -- , if it is money, then it should be there, and it is beautiful. How lovely are thy tents, O Jacob.

If the currency is cattle or grains or flour--, whatever the culture has chosen as valuable, as currency, and as legal tender--, the sacrifices are *supposed* to be there, else the altar will be cold and not functioning.

God, Himself approached man, to make covenant with man. And God decides how broken covenant is to be restored. God has decided that blood is the sacrifice, and the life is in the blood. Money happens to represent the blood, sweat and toil of a man's labor and life.

Put the money on the altar as God requires, respects and expects.

Put Some Respect on Your Name

Altars control everything. Evil altars work by evil sacrifice. Human sacrifices, the killing and offering of human beings to deities, have been practiced by some barbarous nations, and those in occultism.

Your name may be on a satanic altar. Your name may be on a witchcraft altar. Your name may be on an occultic altar. Your name may be on an evil ancestral altar. You know. And, the way you know is if you are going through things that you know you have not done anything to cause what's been coming to you in your life. All the evil, delays, obstacles, losses, and/or hindrances that have been coming to you that you are experiencing is befuddling and frustrating.

How are you answering these problems? It's got to be more than:

- God knows my heart.
- I'm waiting on God.
- I'm believing or trusting God.
- God's got this.

Those are not answers. Those are excuses. They are excuses for doing nothing. Because if you are talking like that you are only talking and not actually doing anything.

The point is, if your name, image, likeness, or anything that represents you is on an evil altar and you have not **put some respect on your own name** by putting your name, your offerings, your sacrifice, your whole person on a more powerful, that is, Godly altar, then you are not doing anything.

The devil is the prince of this world. He has workers of iniquity, evil human agents who may submit your name for evil, calamity, disappointment—whatever…If you don't answer it, then the spirit world will believe that you agree with whatever evil you have been nominated for.

Yes, it is witchcraft.

Yes, it is occultism.

Yes, you are saved. But what are you doing related to sacrifices and powers that are on ungodly altars?

What's on your altar? If it takes an altar to fight an altar, what are you doing waiting on God? God told the patriarchs when, where, and how to build an altar. He didn't say He would come down from Heaven and build it for them---, or for you.

God Says

God established altars and we are supposed to be following that precedent. However, evil folks have been running with it since then. Evil people will build an evil altar any place they want to bring down evil *spirits*. Evil altars abound in the high places.

It is as though God says that altars are the banks of the spirit world, and the sacrifices are the currency. God established that. God did not say we could change it, so we have to work within the parameters set forth for us.

Noah, Abraham, Moses, and Jacob were altar builders, among others. You should be, as well.

God Honors Altars

The Spirit world works by altars, and altars work by sacrifices. Whatever the enemy is sending out against you is worked on an altar – an evil altar. You have an ALTAR, *don't you?* You need one and you need to keep it burning by keeping sacrifices on it.

Most, if not all who are reading this book are aware that they are going through something negative of a spiritual nature. And there are some who have already been *through* and are only reading this book to understand what they went through or confirm that what they thought it was--, it was.

The Ten Commandments are in the Old Testament, we don't throw them out because they are in the Bible, so why have we been convinced to throw out tithing? If you don't tithe, **WHAT IS ON YOUR ALTAR**? If we are to "take up our cross, daily," and a cross IS an altar, then we should have *daily* sacrifices, weekly sacrifices, first fruits and sometimes double sacrifices on Sabbaths and special days. And we are to bring offerings that are unblemished and honor God--, what are we talking about here?

Enter ye in at the strait gate: for wide is the gate, and broad is the way, that leadeth to destruction, and many there be which go in thereat: because strait is the gate, and narrow is the way, which leadeth unto life, and few there be that find it. (Matthew 7:13-14)

Throwing out parts of the Bible will surely not help you *find* GOD.

God told Cain & Abel how to bring sacrifice to Him. Israel sacrificed several times a day. Job sacrificed regularly for himself and his family – and the devil still got to Job—don't be surprised if the enemy's altar is emanating against you if you are not fighting back from *your* GODLY altar.

Praying, yes, but what's on your altar?

In Christ

I am in Christ. I am redeemed by the Blood of the Lamb, I am in Christ, I am in Christ.

I destroy all evil generational altars of my family's foundation, and I appropriate the Altar of Christ Jesus.

I destroy every witchcraft altar working against me in my life, and I raise and appropriate the Altar of Jesus Christ.

In Christ and with Christ, the gates of hell cannot prevail over my family.

In Christ and with Christ, the gates of hell cannot prevail over my family.

In Christ, the gates of hell cannot prevail over my marriage.

In Christ, the gates of hell cannot prevail over my life, over my education, over my career, or over my finances, in the Name of Jesus.

In Christ, the gates of hell cannot prevail over my health and my well-being, in Jesus' Name.

In Christ, the gates of hell cannot prevail over the Blood of Jesus.

I am in Christ, I am in Christ, I am in Christ.

Amen.

Devourer Rebuked

God will rebuke the devourer – when we stop robbing Him in tithes and offerings. Pay your tithes and give your offerings; make your sacrifices unto the Lord!!! God says you rob Him—God does not lie, cannot lie—without tithes and offerings there is nothing on the altar. Unless you believe that you are 100% filled with the Holy Spirit, and you totally know the mind of God and you know exactly what to put on a Godly altar to please God, then just do what He says.

Yes, tender the sacrifice of Christ as your burnt offering, grain offering, thanksgiving offering, peace offering, and especially your sin offering. But where you are supposed to submit yourself completely to God as a living sacrifice you cannot put *yourself* on the altar, so you put something that **represents** you on the altar.

We do not sacrifice **children**.

We do not sacrifice others, never humans, never people.

We don't bring animals for sacrifice – the evil human agents do that on their hidden, occultic, evil altars.

We bring money.

David says I cannot offer to God something that costs me nothing.

We bring money.

We put money on the altar. The thing that *represents* us is money.

Malachi 3 tells us to stop robbing God in tithes and offerings. By the way I treat God you will know my relationship with God, for example, do I rob Him?. By the way I treat people, you will also know my relationship with God. If I rob God, it is so easy to rob people. Don't do that. We need to walk upright before the Lord, sin not, as much as it is in us, by the Holy Spiri; repent quickly and cry out for Mercy.

By the way GOD treats me, you will know that He is GOD. God is a covenant maker and a covenant keeper. He will do exactly what His Word says. This is how we know He is God.

And we need to have something on our altars. Select, individual sacrifices are for God's favor.

Renew the Covenant

You come home on your anniversary or your wife's birthday **without** a gift. Go ahead and forget flowers on Valentine's Day or other days you two observe – and see what happens to you.

Those gifts are sacrifices; those are individual sacrifices for *favor*. Man of God, you want favor from your wife, right? There are designated times where you and your spouse have agreed to give each other gifts. A gift, or honor is expected; if you don't bring one, then the other will feel robbed.

.

Sacrifices on the altar **renew covenant.** Men, women--, people of God: **Renewed covenant means you are going to have a very good night.**

Men, rob your wife and see what <u>won't</u> happen to you.

Do you want to see that look your children will give you if you don't have their gifts on Christmas morning? They even give you a LIST to make sure you don't mess it up.

GOD has given us a *list* of proper sacrifices to bring Him. That list starts in the Old Testament and continues through the New Testament, **AND** it continues in every WORD that proceeds out of the mouth of GOD. God talks to each of us; do what He puts in your heart to do; do what He tells <u>you</u> to do!

Man has a tendency to forget. We consider God the Ancient of Days, and we don't want Him to forget us or forget what we have prayed for; it is one of the reasons why we pray the Word of God, to remind Him of His Word.

LORD, I'm going through something down here, some devourers, evil human agents, wicked powers or **spirits** *are after me. Hey GOD – remember me? Hello? Are you there, God?*

Gifts help people remember you. Tips given to a waiter in a restaurant are **To** **I**nsure **P**roper **S**ervice. Those are individual sacrifices that we give to other people. And, if we give to *people,* then why do we have to be *told* to give to God?

We do believe that God is real, *don't we*? We believe **in** God, *right*? You don't want God saying or thinking, **I love them, they say they love Me, but they don't ever bring Me anything.**

Shall a man rob God?

Over the ages there have been crooked pastors who have inserted themselves in between man and God to take what is intended from man to God for themselves ---, like porch pirates. The worshipper, the giver didn't rob God in those cases, the evil porch pirate pastor (*altar pirate*) did. God will deal with that person.

But if you didn't take anything **to** God's Altar--, even an R&B singer asked, *What have you done for me lately?* Just as the gifts you bring your beloved renew your covenant with him or her, when was the last time you **renewed** covenant with <u>GOD</u>? Israel renewed covenant with God every day, daily, all day and <u>double</u> on the Sabbath.

From time-to-time spouses will have a public ceremony to renew their vows; it's commonplace. Hey, they say keep the home fires burning. That means *keep something on your altar. That is gifts, sacrifices, time, and attention.* Those things renew covenant and keep relationships fresh.

God has promised to keep you, defend you, shield you, protect you, and fight your enemies for you because you two are IN COVENANT. Is there any reason you shouldn't renew covenant with God **every day**? It will definitely make a regular statement to the kingdom of darkness as to where you stand and who you are *with*.

Job made offerings regularly to **UNDO** any evil thing he or his children *may* have done. Are we better than Job?

Living Sacrifices

What's on your altar?

Prayers? *Good.*

Worship? *Good.*

Praise? *Good.*

Study? *Good.*

Fasting? *Good.*

<u>**ALL**</u> OF YOU is supposed to be on that altar, you are to present <u>yourself</u> a living sacrifice, holy and acceptable to God, which is your reasonable service. You are not supposed to present everything *except* what you want to keep for yourself. (The money?)

Your whole soul, your whole mind, your whole heart, and your whole body is supposed to be on that altar --, or the *representation* of all that, as a living sacrifice. The saying, *my body, my life* is for the world. If you're married, your body is your spouse's. If you are saved, your body is **God's body** in this Earth, and you have given your life to Christ and it wasn't even as difficult or as painful as when He gave His life for you. So, we present our bodies or a *representation* of our life—which is the fruit of our labor, *our money.*

On the flip side, the kingdom of darkness puts *representations* of people (effigies) on evil altars, and that is how they manipulate the lives of good people.

Put your money on the Altar of God and defeat the evil machinations and manipulations of evil human agents, so you can live a victorious life.

Deliverance Sacrifice

What you put on an altar **LIVES**. An altar connects the physical realm to the spiritual realm. SPIRIT LIVES FOREVER.

In spiritual warfare, *we* command spirits and powers to **die** and that means that they are stopped from acting against you by a **higher altar, a greater power: God**. The Most High God has the final say over every *spirit*, demon, devil, power, principality, spiritual wickedness, ruler of darkness in high places and every evil spiritual or physical altar any place in the universe.

But until evil altars are stopped, this is why altars from 500 or 1000 years ago are still kicking out curses against you and/or your family –those curses are **alive**, as long as that altar is being serviced. Those curses don't stop until the evil covenants are broken. The power behind whomever or whatever power put the covenant in place is not going to break it because they get tired. These are *spirits* – they don't wear like flesh.

God, the Word of God, someone with authority speaking the Word of God are the only people who can break an evil covenant. That **could** be you; that *should* be you. If not, you should know where to go for help.

Many times, evil covenants are still in effect simply because nobody broke them. Most of the time that is because nobody knew an evil covenant was even in place. Yes, they may have had some clues that something was wrong, but they don't have all the facts and therefore cannot get a full spiritual diagnosis. Then if they don't know everything that's wrong, if one looks in the wrong place for the answer, they will either not find any answer or will find the wrong answer.

For example, if you have a spiritual problem, but you don't look into the spirit for the answer, you may get a natural solution for a spiritual problem, which will prove not to be a solution at all, and may create another whole problem. Or you may not get an answer at all.

So let's say you get all the clues and you realize it is a spiritual problem so you delve deeply into the spirit to find the answer but you don't stick with it – then, you may solve nothing, or make things worse. Getting half delivered may be worse than not seeking deliverance at all.

Sacrifices on your altar, or other **Godly** altar is pivotal to your deliverance.

Living Sacrifice

The altar that Abraham put a
tenth of all on is *how* Abraham tithed *in
Levi*. Abraham gave of his own free will
and he paid it to someone spiritually
higher than himself--, that is he paid to a
**higher altar. Melchisedec, the *Prince
of Salem*.** Once Abraham's sacrifice was
placed on a Godly altar it ***lived***. It was
in the physical but became connected to
the spiritual realm by the power of God
on that altar. And, so it became as a
living sacrifice.

And without all contradiction the less
is blessed of the better. And here men
that die receive tithes; but there he
receiveth them, of whom it is
witnessed that he liveth. And as I may

so say, Levi also, who receiveth tithes, payed tithes in Abraham. For he was yet in the loins of his father, when Melchisedec met him.

As you see, tithing **IS** mentioned in the New Testament in regards to Abraham, *and Levi who receiveth tithes, paid tithes in Abraham.*

If the first fruits be HOLY the lump is holy. (Romans 11:16).

Abraham's tenth became as a **living sacrifice** and it began to multiply and multiply. Abraham was already a rich man, but he became very rich.

Because **you need LIVING MONEY,** not **DEAD PRESIDENTS,** you would be wise to do the same, put your increase on a Godly Altar. Yes, because I'm telling you, but mostly because the Word of God says to do it, and God has probably told you Himself.

Obey.

That means your money needs to be *sacrificed*, if not all of it as in first fruits, at least a *representation* of it in tithes, because the temptation to serve Mammon is too great in the Earth realm. Your money MUST be put on a Godly altar as a living sacrifice to bless you and into your generations as it keeps multiplying.

Anyone who is doing the will of the Lord is *priesting* for the LORD. You don't have to go to Israel to look for a Levitical priest.

Altars are physical and they are spiritual. Be sure the altar you are priesting at, servicing, or placing sacrifices on is of GOD because what you put on it will LIVE and it will either bless you and your generations, or it will bite you and your offspring.

Saints of God, you won't get what God has without doing what God says.

It's about the heart. If you give all you have, but you don't have love for others, you have given nothing; you don't have the Spirit of God.

If you don't have faith toward God, if you are just going through motions, or like Pharisees giving for show--, showing off because you've *got it like that*, God is not impressed and will not run to that.

If you are competing with others, or any other work of the flesh, your *priesting* and sacrifices will most likely come to nothing.

If you have shame because you are not in the $1000 Line, but you give all you have, drop the shame and God will honor your sacrifice.

If you have pride because you are in the $1000, (or more) Line, then your sacrifice may be an abomination to God.

Jesus was impressed with the widow's mite because of what she gave, but we should also consider **that** she gave and *how* she gave. No one is going to give all they have without faith that there will be help from God, there will be more and a good return on the investment. God says some 30, some 60 and some 100-Fold in the offering.

Saints of God giving ALL you have is putting **yourself** on the altar. The widow's mite was not just coins with Caesar's face on it; it became as a living sacrifice. You don't think the widow had any cattle, do you? No bulls, rams, or goats. She gave or sacrificed with what she had, and she put it on a **higher altar**. Remember, a rock can be an altar, the Rock of Ages.

From the end of the earth will I cry unto thee, when my heart is overwhelmed: lead me to the rock that is higher than I.
(Psalm 61:2)

Battles Won

Because of the Altar, and even when you feel overwhelmed, battles will be fought on your behalf and battles will be won. Covenant means the lesser is better off now, because of being connected to the Greater. God makes and keeps covenant and He does that by Godly Altars. Greater is He that is in us than He that is in the world.

Angels of God are waiting on instructions from you to fight your battles *with* you and also for you. This means that you engage the enemy in prayer, and you call on angelic help from the Heavenly Hosts by voicing the Word of God. You don't say any random thing, or some cool slang, you speak the Word of God in prayer.

What translation?

That's between you and God. The Holy Spirit will bring all things back to your remembrance, and that is needful in warfare and in prayer if you do not have a Bible in front of you. The Holy Spirit also interprets our moans and groans that we may not even understand when we pray.

You can't just say, *The Lord will fight my battles*, you have to know it, believe it, say it, pray it, and fight. Once in warfare the Lord showed me a majestic white horse with a mighty warrior on it and other horsemen in array. The understanding was that I should also mount up and fight **WITH** them, not *instead* of them. When you fight, you will win always because God does not lose battles or wars. He always wins, so in Christ, so will you.

Enemies Defeated

Joshua defeated them.

So Joshua defeated Amalek and his
people with the edge of the sword.
(Exodus 17:13)

Then Israel defeated him with the edge
of the sword, and took possession of
his land from the Arnon to Jabbok, as
far as the people of Ammon was
fortified. (Numbers 21:24)

The country which the LORD defeated
before the congregation of Israel is a
land for livestock, and your servants
have livestock. (Numbers 32:4)

The LORD will cause your enemies
who rise against you to be defeated
before your face; they shall come out

against you one way and flee before you seven ways. (Deuteronomy 28:7)

But be wise and know that God was **not** with the people when they disobeyed Him. The Lord gave them up to their enemies when they were idolatrous and in sin.

So, yes, you want to win, yes you want your offerings honored, you want your prayers heard and your sacrifices to mean something to God. As said before *how* you make offerings to God, and *when* you put sacrifices on a Godly Altar is as important as how you do it, what you do, and how you are *priesting* before the Lord.

As well, the altar must be a Godly altar. It is on you not to be tricked or deceived as to what altar you are putting money or any other sacrifice on, using discernment and listening to the Holy Spirit.

Dwell in Safety

I choose to live in safety; that promise is from God. I choose Peace instead of drama. I choose abundance, health and prosperity. I cherish the protection of GOD.

- Altars of the Only Living God, The King Of Glory, Jehovah, El Shaddai, fight for me, in the Name OF Jesus.
- Lord, contend with those who contend with me.
- Father, fight with those who are fighting against me.

GOD says He will fight my battles – and I want that.

Pray the Word of God. Turn the Word into prayers:.

- Lord, visit them with Thunder and Earthquake and great noise, with storm and tempest and the flame of devouring Fire.

Thou shalt be visited of the LORD of hosts with thunder, and with earthquake, and great noise, with storm and tempest, and the flame of devouring fire. (Isaiah 29:6

- LORD, send forth the sword to slay, the dogs to tear, the fowls of heaven and the beasts of the Earth to devour and destroy them.

And I will appoint over them four kinds, saith the LORD: the sword to slay, and the dogs to tear, and the fowls of the heaven, and the beasts of the earth, to devour and destroy. (Jeremiah 15:3)

Altar sacrifices are how and why you're supposed to be connected to God's Holy Altar and that's how you live abundantly and in health. That is **how** you will speak a thing in the physical and it becomes spirit and life because of your connection to **God's Altar** which keeps you in covenant with God, Most High.

One of the spoils of war is the ability to live in safety. That is you will live in both physical and Spiritual safety.

So you shall observe My statutes and keep My judgments, and perform them; and you will dwell in the land in safety.
(Leviticus 25:18)

People fight because their safety is being threatened, or they don't want their safety threatened, so they fight. If you have the opportunity, and I can say luxury of not having to physically fight--, that is, go to war but all you have to do is spiritually serve God and walk that out in your life, then do it. Do it because it is the right thing to do, but do it so you won't ever have to fight in a physical war. Keep the enemies at bay while they are few. Keep the enemies away when they are far away. Do not do nothing and wait until you are surrounded.

Then Israel shall dwell in safety. The fountain of Jacob alone, In a land of grain and new wine; His heavens shall also drop dew. (Deuteronomy 33:28)

Live in Kingdom Abundance

Abundance of finances, health, the prosperity of your words must come from God because there are powers fighting you from getting any or all of that. When you are ministering at your Godly altar God readily hears what you say because He is nearby, nigh thee, even in your mouth.

But what saith it? The word is nigh thee, *even* in thy mouth, and in thy heart: that is, the word of faith, which we preach; (Romans 10:8).

The glory of any battle or war is the spoils. We humans love to win increases and gain more money. Every battle and war you fight and win there are spoils. If you've entered into the fray because of having been ripped off, then you are due 7-fold return of what has been stolen from you. That is spoils, that is glory and it is to the glory of God.

(The men of war had taken spoil, every man for himself.) Numbers 31:53

Now consider how great this man was unto whom even the patriarch Abraham gave a tenth of the spoils. (Hebrews 7:4)

Here's some abundance: when your servants have livestock, God is really blessing you.

The country which the LORD defeated before the congregation of Israel is a land for livestock, and your servants have livestock. (Numbers 32:4)

You fight spiritual wars, you will win, in the Lord. You win, you get spoils. Remember to consecrate the correct portion of all your gains to the

Lord. Where do you put these consecrated gains? On a Godly altar.

The altar is a place of slaying. If what you're putting on the altar is income from your regular job, and not from warfare, it is not called spoils, but it is gains or increase. By virtue of your offerings, the enemies of God will be *slayed* because the sweet-smelling aroma, and your prayers, God will arise. He comes to the place of sacrifice to bring you favor, peace, prosperity, health, and deliverance which all **slays** your enemies; it undocs all the enemy had planned or had initiated against you. You win, and you win again.

It is wiser to sow the seed than to have it stored up in the barn for pests to eat or for it to rot. It is wiser, and it is God's plan that you "sow" your offerings onto the Altar of God so they can prosper for you rather than clutch that money so tightly that you choke it.

Raise Your Home Altar

Find the place where you would like your altar. It may be in a private place in your home, or wherever you would like it. I personally do not want anyone to handle or touch the things on my altar, so I put it in an uncommon area. It's not hidden, it is just not for all eyes and hands to touch. It is a place of consecration, covenant, petition, prayer, dedication, decision.

It is a place of Godly, angelic travel and the powers behind those *spirits*. It's a place of meeting between the natural and the supernatural. When you remove the items on the altar, the powers still linger in that place.

Prayers, fasting and offerings without an altar puts you at a spiritual deficit. Having an altar will allow you to invite Godly angelic spirits on behalf of your needs and requests.

Whether witchcraft altars, marine kingdom altars, occultic altars – you need an altar to fight those altars. Our altar is powered by God so it will be mightier than any of the altars of darkness.

You might choose among these items for your altar that you are setting up:

- Holy Bible, (the version you choose.)
- Anointing oil
- Holy Communion items: Bread & the Blood
- Anointed water (blessed water)
- Pictures of people you pray for.

- Money? That which you will sacrifice to the Lord goes on an altar.

Do not put ungodly, idolatrous, or suspicious items on your altar because you think they are pretty or cool. KNOW that what is on your altar will not draw any demonic *spirits*. NO New Age stuff like crystals and be careful of any candles. Candlemakers and sellers have a full line of demonic candles that have been charmed with intent; do not put that on your Godly altar, no matter how good they smell.

Call your home altar by any name you choose: Restoration, Peace, Victory –, give your altar a name. Wholeness, prosperity, breakthrough, Altar of Fire, are some examples.

Consecrate your altar: dedicate it to the Father, the Son & the Holy Ghost. Bless your altar. You can pray something like this:

Heaven and Earth will bear witness today that I dedicate this altar to the Lord (Name it.). As I dedicate this altar I consecrate it to You, Lord that no weapon, no curse, no infirmity, arrows, hexes, vexes, voodoo, hoodoo, witchcraft, spells, enchantment, conjuration, no other satanic, marine or witchcraft altar, or other territorial altar that would fire against me will be allowed because I am anointed of God. This altar will not allow any curse, invocation or satanic embargo against me, in the Name of Jesus. Thank You, Lord, bless You. My altar is consecrated to the Lord by the Blood of Jesus Christ the power of the Word and the Fire of the Holy Ghost, Amen.

Thank You and bless you and I adore Your Lord, in the Name of Jesus.

Now you may *priest* over your altar. Regularly. Diligence is a big thing with God, be consistent in your prayers, worship, study, and *priesting*.

I come against every evil altar, every strongman that is coming against me, against my destiny, breakthrough, family, calling, career, or finances, in the Name of Jesus.

I crush every altar of wickedness, in the Name of Jesus.

I come against bloodline altars and sacrifices of ancient evil altars, in the Name of Jesus.

The fire on the altar shall be kept burning on it; it shall not go out. (Leviticus 6:12)

Connect to A Greater Altar

Unless you are the great high priest, second only to God--, and you are not--, you need to connect to a greater altar, a higher altar. Everyone does. Yes, you have established your home altar, or your personal altar. In reality, even your dining table is a family altar as you all sit around it together every day, but that does not mean that you don't need a church or should not go to church again. By all means you need to continue priesting at your own altar and your own family altar, but you need to connect to an altar greater and higher than yours.

All of us need to submit to higher authorities than ourselves. At times, we need correction, teaching, admonition prayer and deliverance. We must connect to other saints and bring our gifts, both natural and spiritual, to the Body of Christ. We bring what the Lord has put in us that is *for* the Body.

Do not think that since you have a home altar you don't need to do anything else or connect with any others spiritually. Many folks have home altars already. Maybe you are the one to share with those who don't, and teach them how to consecrate their own personal altar.

I put money on my home altar. That is where it should be until it is transferred to an altar that is **higher** than my own. But that offering, that sacrifice once dedicated and consecrated for God's use has always been separated from my regular money and put on a Godly altar. And that's exactly where it should always be; that's where it belongs. On that altar, the money placed there is connected to the Spirit and it is given *life*. That money is given **life** and power by being sacrificed to the Lord. The sweet-smelling aroma causes God to come to the place of sacrifice to bring what you prayed for and what you need. **Slay** your sacrifice; count it as dead; do not regret the sacrifice, even though it is something desirable to you --, else God wouldn't want it. That sacrifice draws God to your altar. When God arises, your enemies who are also His enemies will scatter!

Obviously, money on your altar that you will give to the Lord, can't just be left there. As part of my giving platform, that money stays on my personal altar until I go into the House of the Lord and can bring it, or until there is a service where that sacrifice can be received, anointed, and prayed over by my pastor. Everyone needs a Godly pastor even popular and high-profile pastors and ministers.

Altar Prayers

Every devil, demon, or spiritual entity, even if you have had legal right into my life, I close every door that has been opened by my ancestors or by my own sin. Lord, forgive me for my own mistakes, in the Name of Jesus, I plead the Blood of Jesus.

My altar is the Cross of Jesus Christ; I tender the sacrifice of Christ as my offering, in the Name of Jesus.

The power that's in the Blood is my defense and my help and my protection, in the Name of Jesus.

Christ, and Him crucified is the power I'm calling on. Lord, let Jesus' sacrifice, and His ascension. work for my life, in the Name of Jesus.

Let the Altar of Jesus speak in my home, in my life, in my family, in Jesus' Name.

I bring down every altar that God said to tear down--, witchcraft, occultism, Satanism, Freemasonry, secret societies, every altar working against me, projecting against me, innovating against me, militating against me. I bring them down by the power in the Blood of Jesus, and I announce and appropriate the altar and the authority of Christ in my life, in my home, my family, and my foundation, in the Name of Jesus.

Thank You for Your New Covenant. Thank You that You are our God and we are Your people and You reconcile Yourself to us, in the Name of Jesus.

Thank You, Lord, for the Better Blood and the New Covenant.

I will not be sacrificed on the altar of witches, in the Name of Jesus.

I will not be sacrificed on the altar of sorcerers, in the Name of Jesus.

I will not negotiate with or at the altar of darkness, in the Name of Jesus.

I will not partake of the altar of darkness or participate on the altar of darkness, in the Name of Jesus.

I am in Christ. I am in Christ. I am in Christ.

Every representation of my resources on satanic altars and demonic covens is retrieved back to me by the Right Hand of the Lord, in the Name of Jesus.

Ancestral debt collector sent to suck the life out of my altar and my destiny, let the Blood of Jesus answer you, in the Name of Jesus.

My name, face, image, likeness, or virtue, tied on any evil altar, is not of

Jesus, in the Name of Jesus, have my picture to catch Fire right now, and my virtues are returned to me. Amen.

The Altar of God shall live, it shall not be desecrated, in the Name of Jesus.

Powers sent to destroy the altars of God be removed and destroyed, in the Name of Jesus.

Every mark of destruction placed upon my life from satanic altars, Blood of Jesus wipe it away, in the Name of Jesus.

I am in Christ, I am in Christ, I am in Christ.

And by the decree of God's altar, I decree that powers bringing my name to any altar of evil and receive the wrath of God, in the Name of Jesus.

Every stone of my ancestors that is set to bring the failure of my ancestors into my life, Altar of God, remove all those stones, in the Name of Jesus.

By the power of God, all powers and affliction shall receive the rod and inherit their own affliction, in the Name of Jesus.

Every incision of darkness that I've submitted to or that someone may have submitted me to, be cancelled by the Blood of Jesus.

By God's altar, I decree the power sending infirmity my way, receive the wrath of God and inherit their own infirmity, in the Name of Jesus.

By God's altar, I decree the power sending paralysis my way, receive the wrath of God and inherit their own paralysis, in the Name of Jesus.

Lord, let the Fire that comes from the Altar of God find any altars promoting death to my life, my spouse, or my children, and burn those altars to ashes, in the Name of Jesus.

Altars showing a representation of me on it for evil, be destroyed by the all-consuming Fire of God's altar, in the Name of Jesus.

Curses by association with *idols* on evil altars, be broken by the Blood of Jesus, and the power of God's altar, in the Name of Jesus.

Altar of God, work for me. Go out, locate anything causing affliction to my spouse and children, and burn those altars to ashes, in the Name of Jesus.

Desecration on the temple of my destiny be cleared off by the name of Jesus.

Evil that has located my life through false altars, let the altar of God uproot and destroy you, in the Name of Jesus.

Implantation of darkness from evil in my life, be uprooted in the Name of Jesus,

Lord Jesus, search the foundation of my life and uproot every altar that should not be, in the Name of Jesus.

Lord Jesus, come into my life and uproot every altar that is hosting demons in my life and let them be destroyed, in the Name of Jesus.

Lord Jesus, come into the foundation of my life and uproot every altar that is not of Yahweh, in the Name of Jesus.

Altars in my foundation zapping my financial life be ripped up and removed by the power in the Blood of Jesus.

I am in Christ. I am in Christ.

Any one of my family that has taken my name and pictures to any evil altar for destruction, your time is up. Your time is up. Your time is up. The Fire of God shall descend on you today, in Jesus' Name.

If I have been scheduled an appointment with untimely death it is canceled right now and forever, by the power in the Blood of Jesus and the Altar of God. Amen.

Altar of darkness in any part of my body be uprooted by Fire, in the Name of Jesus.

Any unintentional evil offering I've ever offered be canceled by the Power in the Blood of Jesus.

Every decision or vow of household altars affecting the plan of God for my life be destroyed by the Blood of Jesus, Jesus, Jesus, Jesus.

Thank You, Lord.

I release myself from every evil altar by the power in the Blood of Jesus, Blood of Jesus. Cover me from the crown of my head to the sole of my feet, in the Name of Jesus.

You, evil altar of bondage be destroyed by the Blood of Jesus.

Evil altar of delay and stagnation, every anti-breakthrough altar be roasted to ashes, in the Name of Jesus.

Lord, open my eyes to see those who are taking my case to the underworld, in the Name of Jesus.

Any sexual altars covering my glory, catch Fire, in the Name of Jesus.

I retrieve my spirit from the altars of evil marine powers, in the Name of Jesus.

I retrieve every bit of my humanity, my spirit soul and body from every evil altar, by Fire and by Force, in the Name of Jesus.

Any evil done against my destiny so far with the powers of evil, be reversed, in the Name of Jesus.

Any problem in my family that is affecting us from any evil altar, be cancelled by the Blood of Jesus.

Every evil altar connecting day and night to work against me, receive Fire and die, in Jesus' Name.

My Father whoever is making evil pronouncements against my family name, let them die, in the Name of Jesus.

Any evil entity that is making evil orders to make us useless in life, Lord, arise and turn them to dust, in the Name of Jesus.

The glory of my life that has been stolen by any evil altar, I recover it by FIRE, in the Name of Jesus.

Evil Goliath that kills, die at the evil altar; I'm not your candidate. Fall down and die, in the Name of Jesus.

Any part of my destiny that has been declared dead by an evil priest, God arise and wake it up, wake it up, by Fire, in Jesus' Name.

Any rituals done against me at any altar, by anyone, unfriendly friends, or any evil human agent, Fire of God expose them with Your Fire, in the Name of Jesus. I speak destruction I burn them to ashes, in the Name of Jesus.

Every evil altar attaching itself to my name, hear the Word of the Lord. depart from that strange altar of blood-sucking demons, in the Name of Jesus.

Every satanic priest monitoring my progress from your evil mirror, go blind by Fire, in the Name of Jesus.

Today I raise an altar of continuous prosperity, in the Name of Jesus.

I am in Christ. I am in Christ. I am in Christ.

Sacrifice of my father's house that has caged generations in my family your time is up, burn to ashes and release our destinies from your alter now, in the Name of Jesus.

I seal these declarations across every realm, age, era, dimension and timeline, past, present, and future, to infinity, in the Name of Jesus.

And I declare, any attacks because of these prayers, decrees, and declarations, backfire 7 times, in the Name of Jesus. And know that I am in Christ and Jesus is Lord, He is in me, and He lives. **AMEN.**

Other books by this author

(the books on finance are pictured, some with links)

AK: The Adventures of the Agape Kid

AMONG SOME THIEVES

Ancestral Powers

Barrenness, *Prayers Against*
https://a.co/d/feUltIs

Battlefield of Marriage, *The*

Beauty Curses, *Warfare Prayers Against*

Behave

Blindsided: *Has the Old Man Bewitched You?*

https://a.co/d/5O2fLLR

Break Free From Collective Captivity

Churchzilla, The Wanna-Be, Supposed-to-be Bride of Christ

Courts of Marriage: Prayers for Marriage in the Courts of Heaven (prayerbook)

Courtroom Warfare @ Midnight (prayerbook)

Curses of Blind Men

Demonic Cobwebs (prayerbook)

Demonic Time Bombs

Demons Hate Questions

Devil Loves Trauma, *The*

Devil Weapons: Unforgiveness, Bitterness,...

The Devourers: Thieves of Darkness 2

Do Not Swear by the Moon

Don't Refuse Me, Lord (4 book series)

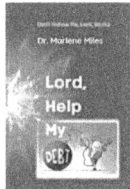

https://a.co/d/idP34LG

Dream Defilement

The Emptiers: *Thieves of Darkness, 1*

Every Evil Bird

Evil Touch

Failed Assignment

Family Token (*forthcoming*)

Fantasy Spirit Spouse

FAT Demons (The): *Breaking Demonic Curses*

The Fold (5 book series)

    The Fold (Book 1)

    Name Your Seed (Book 2)

    The Poor Attitudes of Money (3)

    Do Not Orphan Your Seed (4)

    For the Sake of the Gospel (5)

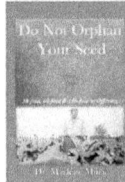

Fruit of the Womb:

Gates of Thanksgiving

Gathered

got HEALING? Verses for Life

got LOVE? Verses for Life

got HOPE? Verses for Life

got money? https://a.co/d/g2av41N

How to Dental Assist

How to Dental Assit2: Be Productive,
Not Wasteful

I Take It Back

Legacy

Let Me Have A Dollar's Worth
https://a.co/d/h8F8XgE

Level the Playing Field

Living for the NOW of God

Lose My Location
https://a.co/d/crD6mV9

Man Safari, *The*

Marriage Ed. Rules of Engagement & Marriage

Made Perfect in Love

Money Hunters: Beware of Those

Money on the Altar

Mulberry Tree, *The (forthcoming)*

Motherboard (The)- soul prosperity series

Name Your Seed

Occupy: *Until I Return*

Plantation Souls

Players Gonna Play

Power Money: Nine Times the Tithe

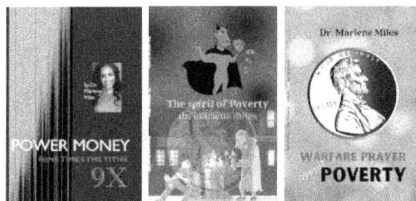

The Power of Wealth *(forthcoming)*

Powers Above

The Robe, Part 1, The Lessons of Joseph

The Robe, Part II, The Lessons of Joseph

Seasons of Grief

Seasons of Waiting

Seasons of War

Second Marriage, Third--, Any Marriage

Sift You Like Wheat

Spirits of Death, Hell & the Grave, Pass Over Me and My House

Soul Prosperity soul prosperity series 3

https://a.co/d/5p8YvCN

Souls Captivity soul prosperity series 2

The Spirit of Poverty

StarStruck

SUNBLOCK

The Swallowers: *Thieves of Darkness*, 3

Take It Back

This Is NOT That: How to Keep
Demons from Coming at You

Throne of Grace: Courtroom Prayer

Time Is of the Essence

Too Many Wives: *Why You Have Lady
Problems*

Tormenting Spirits
https://a.co/d/dAogEJf

Toxic Souls

Triangular Power *(series)*

    Powers Above

    SUNBLOCK

    Do Not Swear by the Moon

    STARSTRUCK

Uncontested Doom

Unguarded Hours, *The*

Unseen Life, *The* (forthcoming)

Upgrade: How to Get Out of Survival Mode

Toxic Souls (Book 2 of series)

Legacy (Book 3 of series)

Warfare Prayer Against Beauty Curses

Warfare Prayer Against Poverty

Wasted, Don't be Defeated by the Waster Spirit: *Thieves of Darkness*, Book 2 (forthcoming)

What Have You to Declare? What Do You Have With You from Where You've Been?

When I Was A Child, I Prayed As a Child

When the Devourer is Rebuked

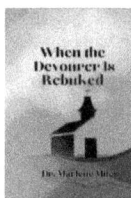

The Wilderness Romance *(series)*

- *The Social Wilderness*
- *The Sexual Wilderness*
- *The Spiritual Wilderness*

www.ingramcontent.com/pod-product-compliance
Lightning Source LLC
LaVergne TN
LVHW051809080426
835513LV00017B/1880